EXPLORING SCIENCE

PLANT CELLS

THE BUILDING BLOCKS OF PLANTS

BY DARLENE R. STILLE

Content Adviser: Irwin Rubenstein, Ph.D., Professor Emeritus,
University of Minnesota, St. Paul

Science Adviser: Terrence E. Young Jr., M.Ed., M.L.S.,
Jefferson Parish (Louisiana) Public School System

Reading Adviser: Susan Kesselring, M.A., Literacy Educator,
Rosemount-Apple Valley-Eagan (Minnesota) School District

 COMPASS POINT BOOKS · MINNEAPOLIS, MINNESOTA

Compass Point Books • 3109 West 50th Street, #115 • Minneapolis, MN 55410

Visit Compass Point Books on the Internet at *www.compasspointbooks.com*
or e-mail your request to *custserv@compasspointbooks.com*

Photographs ©: Ed Reschke/Peter Arnold, Inc., cover, 9; Gary Randall/Unicorn Stock Photos, 4; Digital Vision, 5; Kevin Collins/Visuals Unlimited, 6; Image Ideas, 7; Bob Evans/Peter Arnold, Inc., 8; Corbis, 12; Dr. Richard Kessel & Dr. Gene Shih/Visuals Unlimited, 13; David Fleetham/Tom Stack & Associates, Inc., 14; Rob Curtis/The Early Birders/The Image Finders, 17; Photodisc, 18, 46; OneBlueShoe, 19; Dr. James W. Richardson/Visuals Unlimited, 21; Tom Stack/Tom Stack & Associates, Inc., 22; Ron Holt/ Unicorn Stock Photos, 24; John Gerlach/ Tom Stack & Associates, Inc., 25; A & F Michler/Peter Arnold, Inc., 28; Andre Jenny/Unicorn Stock Photos, 31; Brand X Pictures, 32, 35; Rob & Ann Simpson/Unicorn Stock Photos, 33; USDA/ARS/Scott Bauer, 37; Bettmann/Corbis, 39; Leonard Lessin/Peter Arnold, Inc., 40; Mark E. Gibson/Unicorn Stock Photos, 42; Martha McBride/Unicorn Stock Photos, 44.

Editor: Anthony Wacholtz
Designer/Page Production: The Design Lab
Photo Researcher: Marcie C. Spence
Illustrator: Eric Hoffmann

Art Director: Jaime Martens
Creative Director: Keith Griffin
Editorial Director: Carol Jones
Managing Editor: Catherine Neitge

Library of Congress Cataloging-in-Publication Data
Plant cells : the building blocks of plants / by Darlene R. Stille.
    p. cm. – (Exploring science)
Includes bibliographical references and index.
ISBN 0-7565-1619-6 (hardcover)
1. Plant cells and tissues–Juvenile literature. I. Title. II. Exploring science
(Minneapolis, Minn.)
QK725.S783 2005
    571.6'2–dc22   2005025063

ISBN 0-7565-1764-8 (softcover)

About the Author

Darlene R. Stille is a science writer and author of more than 70 books for young people. When she was in high school, she fell in love with science. While attending the University of Illinois, she discovered that she also loved writing. She was fortunate enough to find a career as an editor and writer that allowed her to combine both of her interests. Darlene Stille now lives and writes in Michigan.

TABLE OF CONTENTS

Cells: The Building Blocks of Plants

THE BRANCHES OF AN OAK TREE spread out from a thick, sturdy trunk. A beautiful rose blooms at the tip of a thin, thorny stem. Tall grasses on an open prairie wave in a summer breeze. Like a mat, soft moss covers a rock on a shady forest floor.

Trees, flowers, grasses, and moss are all plants. Each kind of plant is made of structures that give it a unique shape. Some plants are covered by rough bark, and some have fragrant flowers. Most

plants have roots that go into the soil; other plants, such as mosses and liverworts, do not have roots at all. Botanists, scientists who study plants, are not exactly sure how many species of plants there are in the world. They know that there are more than 260,000 species, and all species of plants are made of plant cells. A cell is the smallest unit of life that provides the basic structure for every living organism.

From the beautiful petals to the sharp thorns, every part of a rose is made up of cells.

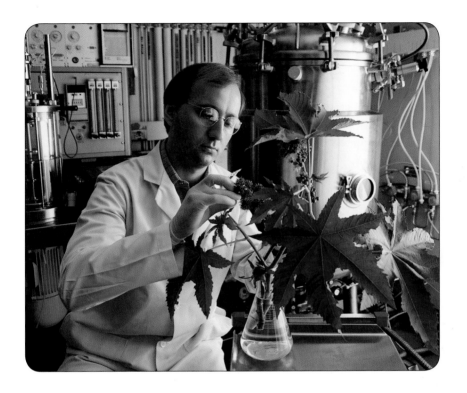

HOW PLANT CELLS ARE LIKE OTHER CELLS

All living things, including animals and one-celled organisms, are made up of cells. Plants, like animals, are made up of trillions of cells. The bigger the plant, the more cells it has. If a plant contains complex parts, it requires additional cells to function as well.

Plant cells, like cells in animals, can group together to form tissues. A tissue is a group of cells that carries on a particular function.

A botanist performs tests on a plant in a laboratory.

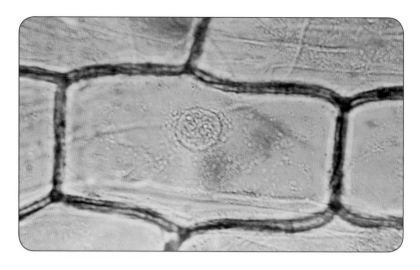

HOW PLANT CELLS ARE DIFFERENT

Plant cells are different from animal cells in two main ways. Plant cells have a stiff cell wall in addition to a flexible cell membrane. Animal cells do not have cell walls. They only have flexible cell membranes.

Cells of green plants, unlike animal cells, contain chloroplasts, which contain a substance called chlorophyll. It allows green plants to make their own food using the energy in sunlight.

The sun's energy is trapped by the plants and becomes part of a process that makes life on Earth possible. Some animals eat plants for food. Other animals eat plant-eating animals. The energy from the sun used by plants to grow is passed along from plant cells to animal cells.

The nucleus and cytoplasm, visible in this onion plant cell, are two of the similarities between plant and animal cells.

It Looks Like a Plant

Leafy seaweed that waves back and forth in the ocean looks like a big underwater plant. It is not. It is a type of algae. All but one species of algae are a type of organism called a protist.

Scientists divide all living things into five major groups, or kingdoms. We are most familiar with the plant and animal kingdoms. The other three kingdoms are made up of organisms called protists, monera, and fungi. The fungi kingdom includes yeasts, molds, and mushrooms. Fungi usually live off of dead or decaying organisms. Most protists are one-celled organisms. While many types of algae are single-celled, others contain many cells.

Algae come in a variety of colors and sizes. There are green, brown, and red species of algae. All algae, like plants, have chloroplasts in their cells to capture the energy of sunlight and make food.

The largest species of algae is a type of seaweed

Although they look like plants, these orange mushrooms are actually fungi.

called giant kelp, which can grow to be 200 feet (60 meters) long. The smallest algae are one-celled organisms such as diatoms and dinoflagellates. Together with microscopic animals, these algae make up plankton. Plankton is crucial to the ocean's food chain and is a major source of Earth's oxygen.

Giant kelp have lumps called gas bladders at the base of each leaf to help keep the plant upright.

CHAPTER TWO

What Plant Cells Are Like ⊕

THE STIFF WALLS of plant cells are made of materials such as lignin and cellulose. Lignin is the substance that makes wood hard and stiff. Cellulose forms fibers in many species of plants.

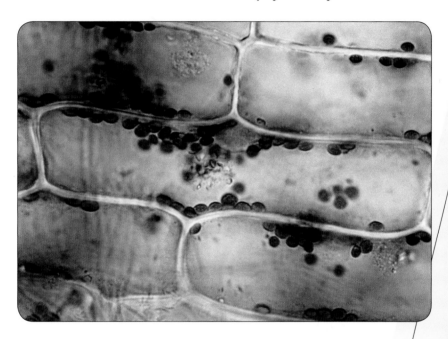

INSIDE A PLANT CELL

Within its cell wall and membrane, a plant cell has two basic parts called the nucleus and the cytoplasm. The cell nucleus contains tiny threads called chromosomes. Chromosomes carry the plant's genes, the basic units of heredity. Genes contain the "blueprints" for what the plant looks like and what the plant cells do.

Under a microscope, the cell wall, nucleus, vacuole, and chloroplasts of this living plant cell are clearly visible.

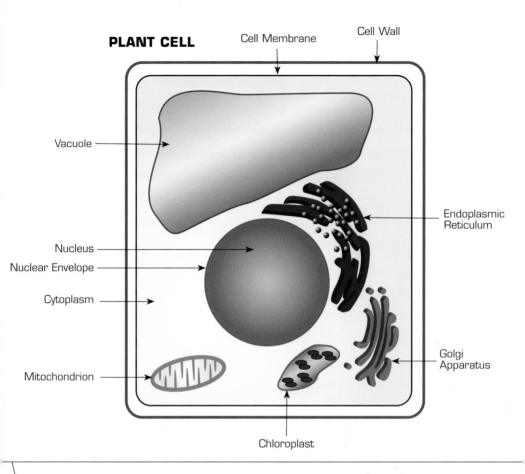

PLANT CELL

Cell Membrane

Cell Wall

Vacuole

Endoplasmic
Reticulum

Nucleus

Nuclear Envelope

Cytoplasm

Golgi
Apparatus

Mitochondrion

Chloroplast

The cytoplasm is a region of the cell that surrounds the nucleus. Several parts in the cytoplasm called organelles do the cell's work. Organelles called the endoplasmic reticulum and the Golgi apparatus "supervise" substances that go in and out of the cell.

PLANT CELL STORAGE TANKS

Within plant cells, there are spaces called vacuoles. They are filled with fluid and provide the cell with food and water storage, among other functions. Many plant cells have a large, central vacuole that helps maintain the cell's water balance. Water in the vacuoles of plant cells makes leaves and other plant parts look plump and healthy. What happens when you forget to water a houseplant? It begins to droop because its vacuoles are out of water.

PLANT CELL POWER PLANTS

Plant cells are busy places and need lots of energy to do their work. Organelles called mitochondria make this energy. The energy comes from a chemical called adenosine triphosphate (ATP). It is made by a complex chemical process that begins when the plant captures the sun's energy. In plant cells, the fuel comes from sugar that the plant makes in its chloroplasts from water, carbon dioxide gas, and sunlight.

DID YOU KNOW?

Mitochondria supply energy to animal cells, too. In animal cells, the mitochondria get the fuel to make ATP from the food the animal eats. Because of the amount of energy needed, there are many mitochondria in animal tissues. For example, large amounts of energy are needed for muscles in the heart to function properly.

Cellulose from Plant Cell Walls

A wooden chair, a linen sheet, and a cotton shirt all have one thing in common: A large part of the materials they are made of contains cellulose.

Cellulose is the principal structural material in the cell walls of land plants. The plants make cellulose from sugar. Cellulose fibers help make roots, stems, and leaves strong. Cotton fiber contains more than 90 percent cellulose, while wood is only 50 percent cellulose.

People use the cellulose from plant cell walls for many purposes. Cellulose fibers in flax and cotton plants make linen and cotton cloth strong. Paper is almost pure cellulose. Cellulose can also be mixed with chemicals to create certain kinds of plastics.

Fruits and vegetables contain cellulose. Although our bodies cannot digest cellulose, the cellulose fibers mix with digested food and provide the fiber that helps our bodies eliminate waste.

Cellulose makes up a large portion of cotton plants.

CHAPTER THREE

What Plant Cells Do

AN IMPORTANT JOB of a plant cell is to make the chemicals a plant needs to live. Cells are like tiny chemical factories. Plant cells combine sugars with minerals and other biochemicals to make vitamins and other chemicals that keep the plant alive.

Plant cells also make chemicals called proteins. Different plant proteins do different jobs. Some proteins help with cell growth and repair. Proteins called enzymes help initiate and speed up many chemical reactions in the plant cell. Structures called ribosomes help assemble proteins.

BASIC PLANT CELLS

There are several kinds of plant cells and tissues. The outermost tissue of leaves, young roots, and stems is the epidermis, usually a layer that is only one cell thick! Epidermal cells create epidermal tissue, which acts like a skin to protect the plant.

Xylem and phloem are tissues that are composed of many different types of cells. The xylem moves water and minerals from the roots to other plant

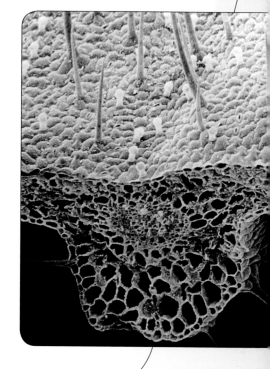

A cross-section shows the layer of epidermal cells layering the outside of the leaf. It also reveals the stomata located within the leaf.

13

parts. Phloem moves food from green cells to cells throughout the plant. Green cells, found mainly in leaf tissue, contain organelles called chloroplasts that use sunlight to make food for the plant.

About 90 percent of the plants in the world are flowering plants. Botanists call flowering plants angiosperms. The main parts of a flowering plant are the roots, the stems, the leaves, and the flowers. Each plant part contains layers of the basic cell types.

The kahili ginger is an exotic flower found in Hawaii.

CELLS IN PLANT ROOTS

Roots hold the plant in the ground and absorb water and minerals. The outer layer of a root is made up of epidermal cells. Some epidermal root cells have thin hairs that stretch out from the cell wall like fingers poking through a balloon skin. The root hairs are actually part of the cell wall. They help the root absorb water and minerals.

The root cap is the tip of the root that pushes deeper and deeper into the soil. Tough epidermal cells make up the root cap. These cells protect the tip and are constantly dying off as the root tip pushes its way through the soil. Root

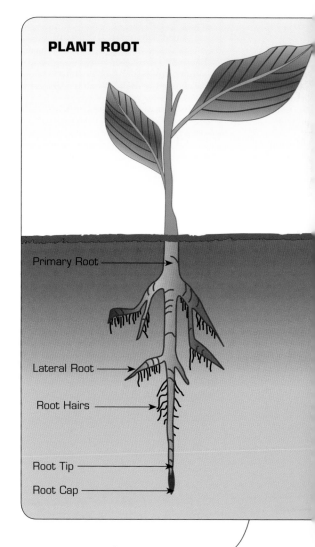

PLANT ROOT

Primary Root

Lateral Root

Root Hairs

Root Tip

Root Cap

cap cells also give off a slimy substance called mucilage. It helps the root slide down through spaces between particles of soil.

Above the tip, roots contain cells that make up xylem and phloem tissues. The xylem carries the water and minerals that have been absorbed from the soil by the root cells. The phloem brings food down to the root cells. Parenchyma cells inside the root store the water and minerals.

CELLS IN PLANT STEMS

The plant stem is the part just above the root. The stems of trees, shrubs, and many other flowering plants grow above ground, but some grasses and other plants have stems that grow under the ground surface. One job of cells in the plant stem is to move water, minerals, and food between the roots and the leaves.

Stems can be either woody or nonwoody. Woody stems are stiff, and they form trunks and branches on trees and shrubs. Nonwoody stems are soft and bend easily. Cattails and other plants that grow in marshes have soft, nonwoody stems. Both woody and nonwoody stems are made up mainly of epidermal cells, parenchyma cells, and xylem and phloem. The difference between woody and nonwoody stems comes from the directions in which the stems grow.

The stems of nonwoody plants grow mainly from new cells that form at the tip of the stem. Tissue that forms at the tips of stems helps with the development of primary growth tissue. Primary growth tissue creates epidermal, parenchyma, xylem, and phloem cells.

Tree trunks, branches, and other woody stems grow both upward and outward. They get thicker every year. These stems contain cells that form secondary growth tissue that increase

Cattails have thousands of tiny brown flowers tightly packed at the end of the stem.

the diameter of the stem. They also contain cells that form primary growth tissue, which increases its length. Secondary tissue is xylem and phloem made by cells in layers called the cambium and the cork cambium. Secondary tissue grows in circular layers around the stem and creates wood and bark. Each year, a tree trunk adds a new ring of secondary tissue growth.

CELLS IN PLANT LEAVES

Like roots and stems, plant leaves have an outer layer of epidermal cells. Epidermal cells in leaves have a waxy coating called the cuticle. Plants that grow in bright sunlight have a thick cuticle to prevent damage from the sun's rays. They also

The number of rings in a tree trunk equals the age of the tree.

have hairs that grow out of the cell wall. Some plants have so many hairs that they feel fuzzy. On the other hand, the epidermal cells of ferns and other plants that grow in dim light have thin cuticles and few cell hairs to let in as much sunlight as possible.

Epidermal cells in leaves also have openings, or pores, called stomata. The stomata take in carbon dioxide from the air. Two guard cells around each stomata open and close the pore.

Water travels up the stem through the xylem and enters

Some plant leaves are covered with tiny hairs, giving them a soft texture.

LEAF CROSS-SECTION

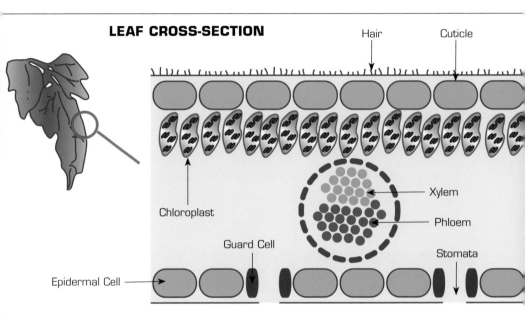

Hair

Cuticle

Chloroplast

Xylem

Phloem

Guard Cell

Stomata

Epidermal Cell

the leaf through a part called the petiole. The petiole is a thick stalk that attaches the leaf to the stem or branch. Water then travels through the leaf in structures called veins. The veins are made up of xylem and phloem cells.

All parts of a plant leaf help with a process called photo-synthesis—making food from water, carbon dioxide, and sunlight. An extremely important process, photosynthesis takes place in two kinds of plant tissue under the epidermis, the palisade tissue and the spongy tissue. Cells in palisade tissue are long and thin, while cells in spongy tissue have an irregular

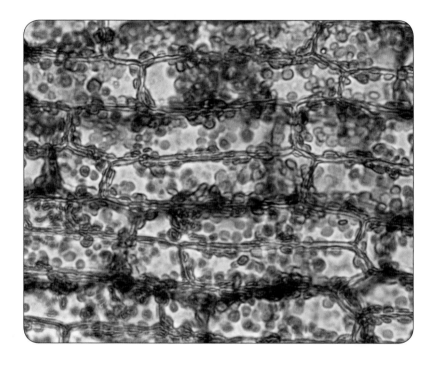

shape. Cells in both kinds of tissue contain many disk-shaped chloroplasts containing chlorophyll, the substance that makes photosynthesis possible.

Water and carbon dioxide surround the cells. Heat from the sun turns some of the water into a gas called water vapor. During photosynthesis, chlorophyll absorbs energy from sunlight. The cells use this energy to split water molecules into atoms of hydrogen and oxygen. The hydrogen and carbon dioxide are combined in the chloroplast to make a sugar, which the plant uses for food. The food travels to all parts

Chloroplasts are vital to the process of photosynthesis.

of the plant through the phloem. The oxygen, a gas that animals breathe, and leftover water vapor are waste products that go out into the air through the stomata. The escaping water vapor cools the leaf in a process called transpiration.

Photosynthesis primarily takes place in the leaves of plants. However, some plants, like cacti, have no leaves. The prickly needles of a cactus plant have evolved to protect its stem from birds and other animals, and there is no green chlorophyll in cactus needles. The chlorophyll-containing chloroplasts are in the cactus stem, which is where photosynthesis takes place.

DID YOU KNOW?

Plant leaves have many stomata for taking in carbon dioxide and giving off oxygen and water vapor. The leaf of a sunflower plant has about 2 million stomata.

Cacti, such as a golden barrel cactus, have prickly needles incapable of performing photosynthesis.

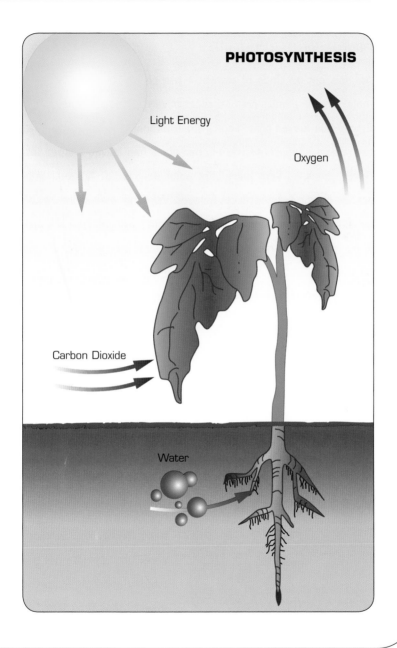

PHOTOSYNTHESIS

Light Energy

Oxygen

Carbon Dioxide

Water

Plants that Eat Animals

Animals eat all kinds of plants. A few plants, however, eat animals! These plants are called carnivorous plants. The Venus flytrap has leaves that hinge. When an insect enters the plant, the leaves snap shut. The pitcher plant has leaves shaped like tubes and lined with hairs that point downward. A sweet substance on the tube attracts insects. When an insect enters the tube, the downward-pointing hairs keep it from getting back out. The sundew plant has sticky hairs that capture insects that land on them.

All carnivorous plants give off juices that digest the insects, but the plants do not use the insects as their main food. Chloroplasts in the plant cells make food by photosynthesis. All carnivorous plants, however, live in places where the soil is poor in nitrogen and other minerals that plants need to grow. Instead, carnivorous plants get the needed minerals from the insects that they "eat."

Two Venus flytraps fight over dinner.

How Plants Reproduce

COLORFUL FLOWERS are more than just pretty parts of plants. Flowers play a key role in creating the cells that develop into new plants. Flowers contain the parts that a flowering plant needs to reproduce sexually. Evergreen trees have reproductive parts in their cones. Some plants, such as ferns, don't have flowers. The reproductive parts of ferns are on the leaves.

White spruce cones are actually flowers and contain the tree's reproductive parts.

Most flowering and nonflowering plants make both male and female sex cells. The two sex cells, pollen and eggs (ovules), join to eventually make a whole new plant.

Both flowering and nonflowering plants also make cells that cause the plant to grow and to replace cells that die. These cells are called somatic cells. New somatic cells form on the tips of the roots pushing down into the ground. These cells form buds on the tips and sides of the stems and branches growing upward. The places on plants where new somatic cells grow rapidly are called the apical meristems. New cells also form in the cambium of woody plants.

Both somatic cells and sex cells are created by cell division. The two kinds of cells, however, divide in different ways called mitosis and meiosis.

DID YOU KNOW?

An apple, cherry, or other fruit is a swollen ovary, a female part at the bottom of a flower's pistil. The layers of the fruit protect one or more seeds inside.

MITOSIS IN PLANT CELLS

Somatic cells divide by mitosis. During mitosis, a cell divides in half to make two daughter cells. Each daughter cell has identical traits passed on by its genes. The chromosomes that

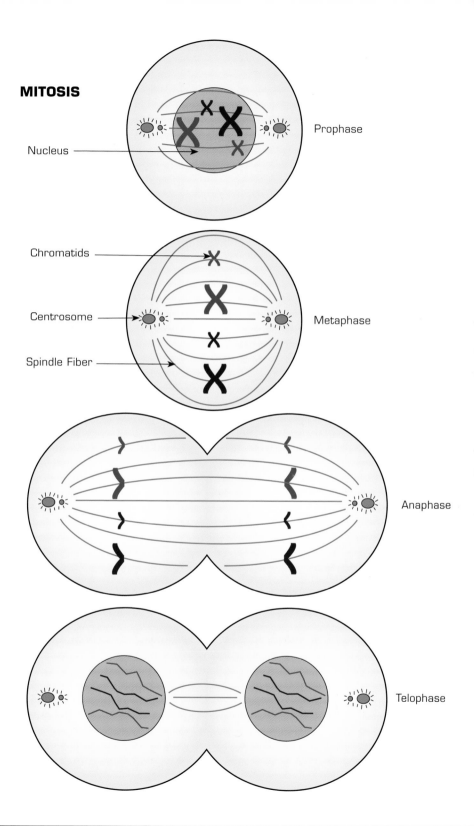

MITOSIS

Nucleus

Prophase

Chromatids

Centrosome

Metaphase

Spindle Fiber

Anaphase

Telophase

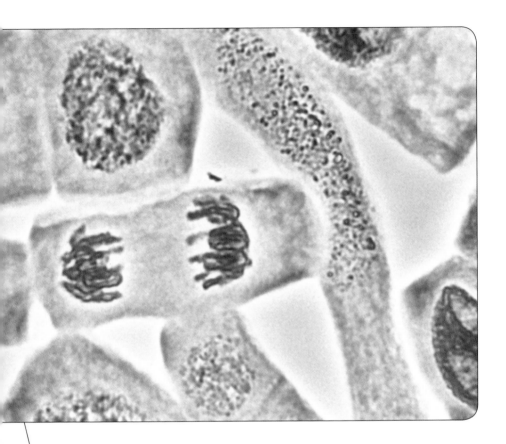

carry genes in somatic plant cells occur in pairs, one chromosome from each parent. Before a cell divides in two, its chromosomes and genes must divide.

Mitosis begins when the chromosomes make copies of
themselves. The copies, called sister chromatids, are joined
in the middle, giving them an "X" shape. A structure made
of protein fibers, which is called a spindle, forms in the

An onion root tip cell during the anaphase stage of mitosis

center of the nucleus. The middle of the spindle is called the equator. The chromosomes line up on the spindle with each sister chromatid on opposite sides of the equator. The sister chromatids then separate and move toward opposite ends of the spindle, where they become new chromosomes. A nuclear membrane forms around each set of chromosomes. The cytoplasm pinches together between the nuclei, forming the two daughter cells.

MEIOSIS IN PLANT CELLS

Sex cells are formed by a different type of cell division called meiosis. During meiosis, a cell duplicates its chromosomes once and then goes through two cell divisions. The first cell division makes two new daughter cells, each with a complete set of chromosomes. During the second division, the daughter cells divide to create the sex cells with only one set of chromosomes each. When a male and female sex cell join, they create a new cell (the zygote) with a complete set of chromosome pairs.

ALTERNATION OF GENERATIONS

Sexual reproduction in most plants occurs through a complex series of steps called alternation of generations. There are two phases: the gametophyte phase and the sporophyte phase.

MEIOSIS

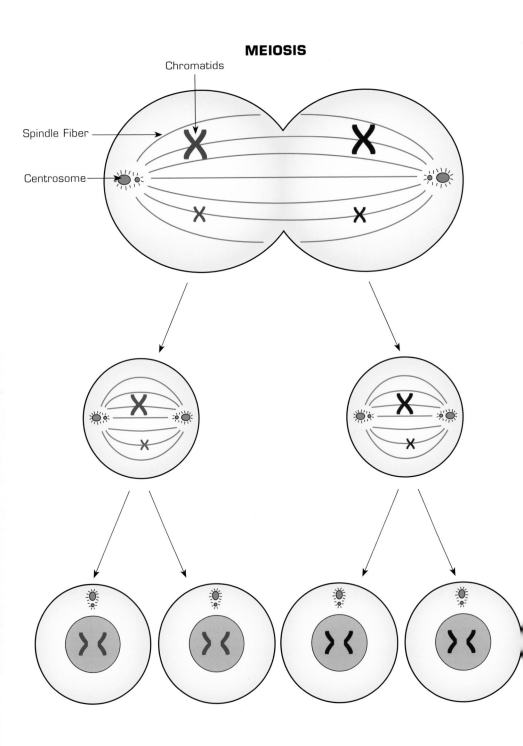

In most plants, sporophytes are the form that looks familiar to us. Rose bushes, maple trees, and blue spruce are examples of sporophytes. Gametophytes of most plants live in the reproductive parts of the sporophyte and can only be seen under a microscope. However, the moss gametophyte can be seen and looks like thick mats of moss. The moss sporophyte is a stalk that sticks up above the gametophyte. In ferns, the two phases exist as separate plants, but the gametophyte is very tiny.

Sporophytes, such as maple trees, create a colorful display in the fall.

The cycle begins when cells in the male and female reproductive parts of the sporophyte divide by meiosis to make the sex cells. In flowers, the female part is called the pistil, and the male part is the stamen. In cone-bearing plants, the male and female parts are in different types of cones. The sex cells in the female parts of all plants develop into female gametophytes, which divide by mitosis to produce egg cells inside structures called ovules. The sex cells in the male parts of plants develop into male gametophytes called pollen.

A stargazer lily shows the pistil (middle stalk with an orange bulb) and the stamen (surrounding stalks with maroon tips).

The sporophyte phase of flowering plants and cone-bearing plants, such as pine, spruce, and fir, comes from seeds. To make seeds, pollen must travel from the male reproductive parts to the female reproductive parts of the plant. In some flowering plants, hummingbirds, bees, and other insects carry the pollen from the stamen to the pistil. In cone-bearing plants, the wind blows the pollen from a male cone to a female cone. An egg inside an ovule that is fertilized by a pollen grain develops into a seed, which can then grow into a new plant.

A ruby-throated hummingbird aids in plant reproduction.

Plant Clones

Plant clones are everywhere. We enjoy flowers from plants that have been cloned. We eat fruits and vegetables from plants that have been cloned.

Plant clones are created by a form of asexual reproduction called vegetative propagation. No sex cells are involved in asexual reproduction. Plants produced by asexual means have the exact same genes in all their cells as the parent plant—they look identical. Offspring with identical genes are called clones.

Plants reproduce asexually when new plants grow from existing plant parts. New plants can bud from special underground stems called bulbs, corms, rhizomes, and tubers. Irises, violets, and some grasses bud from underground rhizomes that spread outward from the parent plant. Tulips bloom in the spring from bulbs, and gladiolas grow in summer from corms buried in the soil. A new plant can even be cloned in the laboratory from a single plant cell.

For centuries, gardeners have used vegetative propagation to grow the kinds of plants they want. They take pieces of leaves, roots, and stems and use them to grow whole new plants. Fruit growers graft, or attach, a bud or branch from a tree that produces wonderful fruit to the root or stem of a tree already growing. The graft grows out from the stem and produces fruit like that found on the original tree. Many

fruits, such as Macintosh apples, can only be grown from such grafts.

Vegetable gardeners often grow new potato plants from pieces of cut-up potato. Potatoes are tubers, thick underground parts of a stem. Each piece of planted potato must contain an eye, or bud, in order for a new plant to grow.

Violets multiply through a form of asexual reproduction.

⊕ Studying Plant Cells

BECAUSE CELLS ARE SO SMALL, botanists must study them under microscopes. Even under a microscope, the organelles inside plant cells are difficult to see. Botanists use different kinds of dyes or stains to color different organelles inside the cells so that they show up more clearly under a microscope.

WHY SCIENTISTS STUDY PLANT CELLS

Botanists study plant cells to learn about plant diseases and how to treat them. Fungi, bacteria, viruses, and other microorganisms can cause diseases by attacking plant cells. Some diseases prevent chloroplasts in leaf cells from carrying out photosynthesis. Some diseases block the tubelike cells in the xylem and phloem, preventing food and water from flowing through the plant. Some microorganisms kill off plant cells, causing fruits and vegetables to rot. Plant cells can also be harmed by a lack of minerals in the soil and by chemical pollutants.

Botanists can fight plant diseases by breeding plants that have the traits of an ideal plant. Suppose a type of corn is resistant to a disease, but it does not taste very good. Another type of corn plant tastes great but can easily be harmed by the disease. Scientists can use the sex cells of the two plants to breed a new variety of corn. They take pollen from the resistant

A plant technician checks on futuristic peach and apple "orchards." Each dish holds tiny experimental trees grown from lab-cultured cells into which new genes were inserted.

plant and place it on the pistil of the good-tasting plant. The sperm and egg cells unite to produce a new variety of hybrid corn that both tastes good and is resistant to disease.

DID YOU KNOW?

Many of the chemicals that plants produce can be useful to humans. Plants provide raw materials for fabrics, medicines, and many other products. Botanists study these chemicals to find new uses for them. For example, some plant chemicals are used to treat specific types of cancer.

HOW PLANTS TEACH SCIENTISTS

By studying plants, scientists have learned a great deal about cells and genes. Plant cells were the first cells that scientists discovered. In 1665, an English scientist named Robert Hooke cut a very thin slice of cork and looked at it under a microscope. What he saw looked like holes inside walls. Hooke named these holes "cellulae."

The science of genetics started with studies using pea plants. An Austrian monk named Gregor Mendel studied what happened when he bred and crossbred peas in his monastery garden. Some peas had wrinkled skins, while others had smooth skins. Some plants were short, and others were tall.

Mendel observed the traits in new pea plants bred from similar or different parents. When he crossed short and tall plants, for example, he found that all of these first-generation plants were tall. However, when he crossed the first-generation plants, he

Gregor Mendel analyzed flower petals in his monastery garden.

got both tall and short plants in the ratio of three tall plants to one short plant.

By observing patterns in the different generations of peas, Mendel learned about the laws of inheritance. He theorized

Genetic engineers are able to produce grapes that are much larger than normal.

that each trait was passed along by some heredity unit in the male and female sex cells. He was right, and these units are now called genes.

Botanists still crossbreed plants to get new plants with desirable traits. But a relatively new technique has been discovered. Biologists now know how to insert genes for new traits into the sex cells of certain plants. This technique is called genetic engineering. Genetically engineered food plants might, for example, yield more nutritious fruits or vegetables.

Genetically engineered foods, however, have raised safety concerns. Some people wonder whether putting genes into the chromosomes of plant cells could cause harm in unknown ways. Could the new gene cause unknown changes in other parts of the plant—changes that might be dangerous to people who eat it?

Biologists continue to learn new things about plant cells. They have found, for example, that some plant cells contain a protein substance like hemoglobin called leghemoglobin. Hemoglobin is very important in animals; it carries oxygen in the blood. Leghemoglobin is found in the root nodules of plants like peas and beans. These plants are capable of obtaining the nitrogen they need for growth from the air. Leghemoglobin plays an important role in this process.

Many questions about plants still remain. There is much to be learned by the scientists of tomorrow about plants and their cells.

A researcher examines experimental hybrid citrus plants in a greenhouse.

Pollen and Allergies

Sneezing, a runny nose, and red, swollen eyes can be symptoms of allergic reactions. An allergic reaction is caused by our bodies being too sensitive to various substances. Pollen from plants is usually the culprit in a kind of allergic reaction called hay fever.

Hay fever attacks occur mainly during the summer and fall, when plants are producing pollen. People breathe pollen into their noses and throats. The tiny grains cause an allergic reaction in those who are sensitive to pollen. The reaction comes from our germ-fighting immune system. The immune system mistakes the pollen grains for foreign substances like germs and produces chemicals that cause the symptoms of hay fever.

Any kind of pollen can cause hay fever, but pollen from the ragweed plant is the most common cause. Ragweed grows all over North America. Its pollen is spread by the wind, so ragweed pollen can fill the air. Many people begin sneezing when there are 26 grains of pollen per cubic yard (20 grains per cubic meter) of air. This measurement is called the pollen count. Many radio and television stations broadcast the pollen count on summer and fall days.

When the pollen count is high, people with hay fever should stay indoors as much as possible. Doctors treat hay fever with pills and nasal sprays containing drugs called antihistamines.

In severe cases, doctors can give sufferers injections of the pollen that causes the problem to decrease the individual's sensitivity. Medical scientists are looking for better ways to prevent or treat allergies caused by pollen.

There are 35.9 million people in the United States who are allergic to the pollen in ragweed.

cell wall—material that encloses a plant cell

chlorophyll—chemical that plants use to capture the energy in sunlight

chloroplast—chlorophyll-containing organelle

chromosome—threadlike structure in the nucleus that carries genes

cuticle—waxy coating on epidermal cells in leaves

cytoplasm—part of the cell outside of the nucleus

epidermal cell—cell that forms the protective outer layer of a plant

gene—basic unit of heredity

meiosis—two-stage cell division that produces sex cells with one set of chromosomes each

mitochondria—organelles in a cell that convert energy from one chemical form to another

mitosis—cell division process that creates two new, genetically identical cells

nucleus—the command center of the cell that gives instructions to the other parts of the cell

parenchyma cell—cell with large vacuoles that store food and water

phloem—plant tissue made of tube-shaped cells that carries sugar to stems, roots, and other plant parts

photosynthesis—process that occurs in chloroplasts by which plants make food using sunlight, carbon dioxide, and water

pistil—female reproductive part in a flower

pollen—grains containing sperm produced by a plant's male organs

somatic cell—body cell; any cell except a sex cell

stamen—male reproductive parts in a flower

stomata—leaf pore that lets in carbon dioxide and gives off oxygen

vacuole—large space in a plant cell that stores water and food

xylem—plant tissue made up of tube-shaped cells that carries water and minerals up from the roots

▸ Cork comes from the bark of the cork oak tree. Cork is used for bottle stoppers, fishing floats, insulation, and many other products.

▸ Angiosperms, or flowering plants, come in all sizes. The biggest angiosperms are eucalyptus trees, which can be more than 300 feet (91 meters) tall. Duckweed that floats on ponds is the smallest angiosperm at 1/50 inch (0.5 millimeter) in length.

▸ Bamboo is a tall grass that has a rigid, woody stem. Many people in Asia use bamboo as a building material.

▸ The African raffia palm has the largest leaves and flowers of any plant in the world. Its leaves can grow to be 65 feet (20 m) long, and its flowers can be more than 3 feet (91 centimeters) wide.

▸ Not all plants make their own food. Parasitic plants, such as the dodder, live off of other plants. The mistletoe is called a partial parasite because it makes some of its own food but also lives off of the tree on which it grows.

▸ The wall of an ovary of mature fruit, in which the seed is fully developed, has three layers. The outer layer is called the exocarp, the middle layer is known as the mesocarp, and the inner layer is the endocarp. The three layers together are called the pericarp.

▸ Botanists classify fruits into two main groups: simple fruits and compound fruits. A simple fruit develops from a single ovary, and a compound fruit develops from two or more ovaries.

▸ As a genetic engineering experiment, scientists inserted a firefly gene into a tobacco plant. When it was sprinkled with water containing the energy chemical ATP, the plant glowed in the dark.

All of the fruits we eat are classified as either simple or compound.

At the Library

Kalman, Bobbie. *Photosynthesis: Changing Sunlight into Food.*
New York: Crabtree Publishing, 2005.

Rhodes, Mary Jo, and David Hall. *Life in a Kelp Forest.* New
York: Children's Press, 2005.

Snedden, Robert. *Plants & Fungi: Multicelled Life.* Oxford:
Heinemann Library, 2002.

Spilsbury, Louise, and Richard Spilsbury. *Green Plants: From
Roots to Leaves.* Chicago: Heinemann Library, 2004.

On the Web

For more information on **Plant Cells,** use FactHound to track
down Web sites related to this book.
1. Go to *www.facthound.com*
2. Type in a search word related to this
   book or this book ID: **0756516196**
3. Click on the *Fetch It* button.
FactHound will find the best Web sites for you.

On the Road

The North Carolina Arboretum
100 Frederick Law Olmsted Way
Asheville, NC 28806-9315
828/665-2492
www.ncarboretum.org

Missouri Botanical Garden
4344 Shaw Boulevard,
St. Louis, MO 63110
800/642-8842
www.mobot.org

Explore all the books in this series:

Animal Cells: Smallest Units
of Life
ISBN: 0-7565-1616-1

Chemical Change: From
Fireworks to Rust
ISBN: 0-7565-1256-5

DNA: The Master Molecule of Life
ISBN: 0-7565-1617-X

Erosion: How Land Forms,
How It Changes
ISBN: 0-7565-0854-1

Genetics: A Living Blueprint
ISBN: 0-7565-1618-8

Manipulating Light: Reflection,
Refraction, and Absorption
ISBN: 0-7565-1258-1

Minerals: From Apatite to Zinc
ISBN: 0-7565-0855-X

Natural Resources: Using and
Protecting Earth's Supplies
ISBN: 0-7565-0856-8

Physical Change: Reshaping
Matter
ISBN: 0-7565-1257-3

Plant Cells: The Building Blocks
of Plants
ISBN: 0-7565-1619-6

Soil: Digging Into Earth's Vital
Resources
ISBN: 0-7565-0857-6

Waves: Energy on the Move
ISBN: 0-7565-1259-X